Tao Teh King

by

LAO TZŬ

老子道德經

Tao Teh King

by

LAO TZŬ

▪

A Tentative Translation
:: from the Chinese ::

by

Dr. Isabella Mears

▪

THEOSOPHICAL PUBLISHING HOUSE LTD.
68 Great Russell Street, London, WCIB 3BU
ADYAR, INDIA   WHEATON, ILL.–U.S.A.

First Edition *1922*
Reprinted *1949*
Reprinted *1971*

ISBN 7229 0300 6

Printed in Great Britain by
Fletcher & Son Ltd, Norwich

INTRODUCTION

IT would be difficult, in a short introduction, to give a scheme of the leading thoughts in the Tao Teh King. A few of these are indicated; but it is suggested that the chief use of the book will be found in meditation upon the chapters. The student of Lao Tzŭ will then discover that the book has to do with Life. As he dwells in the pure and lofty conceptions of the ancient sage, he will come to a new view of the circumstances and the meaning of his own life; and he will get a better understanding of the wholeness and the perfectness of the Cosmic Life.

The name "Lao Tzŭ" means "old young," so that on the very threshold of our study we find a paradox, and we may call the wonderful teacher "the old philosopher," "the old child," or "the young old man." His family surname was Li, and the date of his birth is said to have been 604 B.C.

There are many stories about his miraculous birth, his wisdom in youth, and his activity in old age.

In the words " Lao Tzŭ " we seem to catch the throb of Life. He is old, yet young ; old in years and young in heart and mind. In him old age and youth are correlated and interdependent. To him old age is imperfect without youth. Youth holds the bud and promise of the flower and fruit which come through age.

He wrote this book, " Tao Teh King," a book around which cluster much speculation and much literature in Chinese and in other languages.

In the title of the book which has made the fame of Lao Tzŭ we find another paradox, and as we read through his 81 short chapters we continually find truth set forth in quaint, forcible, paradoxical statement.

The word " King " we may leave out of count, as it simply means classic, and was not given by Lao Tzŭ himself, but was added much later as a mark of respect.

In the name " Tao Teh " there again seems to be the throb of vital force. This name has in it the idea of rest and then action, of cause and then effect, of life and then its manifestation, of principle and then the exemplification of principle in action ; these ever recurring, continually. " Tao " —the stream of Life-consciousness ; and " Teh," the unfolding of the Life. We find a whole vision of Life pictured in these two characters.

The word " Tao " has received various inter-pretations, such as " The Way," " The Path," " Nature," " Reason," and many others. The great difficulty in regard to the understanding of its meaning and to giving it a name has always been that Lao Tzŭ seemed to give it, as it were, a paradoxical character. In one chapter he speaks of it as Creator of Heaven and Earth, as existing before God, and in other places he describes it as the very sum of negatives. It has therefore seemed that the only way to gain any sure idea as to the meaning of Lao Tzŭ would be to try to clear the mind of the views of previous commen-tators and translators and to go back to the text, which claims to be a genuine relic of the famous philosopher. If we then take to pieces the character 道 for Tao in order to discover the meaning of its component parts, we find at the left side 辶 , and the dictionary tells us that this means going on and halting, or walking with a measured step. Evidently we may conclude that the underlying idea is that of *progression*. The right hand side of the character is built up by slight unimportant-looking marks from a character meaning eye to one meaning intelligence, thus :— 目 eye, 自 self, 百 head, 首

intelligence. In the final form we note two little marks which in themselves mean " flame," or " influence," coming down from above. We now take the character 道 Tao and clearly see that it holds a possible meaning, that of " *progressive intelligence.*" We find a corroborative expression of the same idea in Troward's Universal Spirit, whose primary quality is that of progressive creative thought ; in Edward Carpenter's glorious Freedom, with its twin Joy beginning but without ending ; and in Henri Bergson's philosophy. The strength of the urge of the " *élan vital* " is being felt in the hearts of multitudes of men and women at this present moment, and is being manifested in a way that is expressed in Lao Tzŭ's next character in the title of his book, 德 Teh, usually translated virtue, but having the dictionary meaning of " principle exemplified in action."

The character 德 Teh, complex-looking, but made up of simple elements, bears in itself its own meaning. The left side of the character is 彳 a short step. On the right side, from above down, we have 十 ten, 目 eye, — contracted from 丌 a bench or firm basis ; the three together reading " What ten eyes see is firmly established " —*i.e.*, truth. Further, when truth is in the 心 heart of man it cannot fail to manifest itself in good

action in his life. So our title " Tao Teh " may
be translated " Life-consciousness and its manifestation in action."

The book has been translated and discussed
by learned men of many nations during many
years. It may seem presumptuous that one
humble student of Chinese should venture to set
forth another translation, and anew attempt to
unravel the difficulties which have puzzled wise
men. The only excuse is that in an honest attempt
to fathom the meaning of Lao Tzŭ by such a
dissection of some of his puzzling characters,
and by the use of such a method as is here indicated, the translator has seemed to gain a light,
a joy and a depth of meaning in the book, that it
is impossible to keep them to oneself. A whole
world of meaning, for instance, has come through
pondering and meditation on the character 無
wu, which has always been translated " not,"
" without," " emphatic negative." The whole
philosophy of Lao Tzŭ seems to turn upon the
real meaning of this character. If you mention
the name of Lao Tzŭ to students of ancient
sacred writings they will say :—" Oh ! Lao Tzŭ.
He taught wu wei, ' not striving.' "

But, in reality, did Lao Tzŭ teach negation,
passivity, non-activity, not striving ?

The character 無 wu, indeed, from its aspect is well fitted to be a symbol of an emphatic not ; but it may have had, in the mind of Lao Tzŭ, a meaning very different.

It seems to be built out of the characters 亻 man, 仁 humanity, 十 ten, symbolic of spirit entering into matter. 十 is three times repeated 卅, and this triple cross is set into the midst of the symbol for humanity, seeming to picture in a few crude lines a tremendous truth, a truth that Isaiah of Palestine taught in the word " Immanuel " about 100 years before Lao Tzŭ lived and taught in China. The four little marks at the foot of the character mean fire, and indicate the influence which comes, which must come, from every Spirit-filled man.

If this be a correct reading of the character 無, then wu wei cannot mean " not striving," but, on the contrary, " striving through the power of the Inner Life."

In reading the Chinese text of the Tao Teh King we find this same 無 wu joined to knowledge, desire, etc., and the translation has been " He (the sage) constantly (tries to) keep them without knowledge and without desire, and, where there are those who have knowledge, to keep them from presuming to act (on it) " (see Prof. Legge's

translation, ch. 3). Instead of which, if we translate wu by "Spirit in man" or "inner life,"
we have a tremendous vital force in the words
"He always teaches the people to know the
inner life, to desire the inner life. He teaches
the masters of knowledge to cease from activity,
to act through activity of the inner life."

One more character must be referred to, it is
that of 有 yu, which means "to have" or
"possession." This is composed of two characters
ナ hand, and 月 moon. The whole character
有 therefore stands for the idea of "holding
the moon," or holding outward possessions
which are in their nature limited and elusive.
有 yu comes in the first chapter of the book
into abrupt contrast with 無 wu. The two
ideas, inner life and outward possession, form
the paradox of this chapter. As with youth
and age, as with Life and its manifestation,
so inner life and outward possession are correlated and interdependent, one in source,
together existent in vital force. And they form
in their relation to each other an expression of
the throb of Life, the pulsation that is inseparable
from Life, the pulsation that goes on continuously
throughout Life.

The theme of "Life and the Manifestation of
Life" pervades the book. Many chapters are

devoted to the qualities of Tao or Life. It is described as Unnameable, Infinite, Inexhaustible ; Sustainer, Preserver of all beings ; Spiritual Form of form. It is always in motion, always undoing, becoming, rebuilding. It extends everywhere, to the left and to the right. Indwelling in the Small, informing the Great, never claiming to be Ruler ; It gives freedom and power of development to all beings.

Tao gives Life to all beings. Teh gives to each one its Form. Tao gives the inward urge towards perfectness. Teh is the Expression or Name of Tao. By yielding to the influence of Tao men will be transformed from within themselves. Its effect is to be observed not only in the physical but in the moral kingdom. Through Tao is maintained the Unity of Prince and people. It unites Heaven and Earth harmoniously to produce the sweet dew. It gathers the people in the bonds of time and individuality. He who knows how to rest in it will never pass away.

Tao is remote and inexpressible, yet ever expressing Itself. Tao is empty ; yet, in the using of It, It is found to be inexhaustible. Tao is invisible ; yet It shines through all things visible. In Tao is stillness ; yet It is the source of unceasing activity. Tao is the well-spring of health and of never-ending life. Teh is the manifestation of life, which is forever seeking its highest expression in Tao. It returns into Tao (ch. 40), and is ever anew sent forth. In this way is formed the Rhythm of Life, with its unceasing throb and rest, eternally, progressively expressing itself.

Intervening chapters tell, in varied metaphor and illustrative picture, the story of the adventure of the human soul in its endeavour to come again into fulness of Tao. Beauty, cleft asunder, is ugliness ; love, cleft asunder, is hatred ; yet in each case the two, interrelated, are in effect parts of one Whole. Human relationships are viewed from a spiritual standpoint. Filial piety itself, crowning virtue in the Chinese mind, is only of value if it comes from the heart. Man is considered as a spiritual being, with power to function from the spiritual plane ; and there are repeated allusions to the endlessness of his real Life : "He who fails not to find the Self shall endure. He who dies but does not perish shall endure for ever."

Another great lesson taught by Lao Tzŭ is that Form has "profit," but that "usefulness" is in the empty innermost. He gives quaint, every-day examples of this teaching, as the hub of a wheel, the empty space within a bowl, and the empty space that is left in a wall for doors and windows. But his inference is that our bodies

are our Form, and that within each one of us
there is room for the indwelling of the Heavenly
One, known vaguely to him as Tao, but more
intimately known also as Heavenly Love. He
says :—" Let Heavenly Love fill you and overflow in you, not according to your measure of
fulness."

It is said that the Tao Teh King was written
when Lao Tzŭ was over ninety years of age.
After a long life as librarian and teacher, and
having met with little response in the lives of
the people, he was on his way to a Place of Rest.
On his way he had to go through a mountain pass,
and there he was for a time the guest of a soldier-
disciple, Warden of the Pass. This friend asked
him to write down, before disappearing for ever
from their midst, some of the lessons he had taught
to his disciples. The book seems to bear in its
heart the influence of that upland valley. The
Spirit of the Valley made itself felt as the real
source of existence, Mother-substance of the Deep,
Preserver and Nourisher of all beings. There he
saw men who were timid at crossing a torrent in
winter. There the winds brought to him their
message of the unseen Power, that " emptied,
loses not power. Moved, it sends forth more and
more wind." Again, we seem to see the aged,
clear-minded Sage sitting looking at the water,
always so busily seeking for itself a lower place,

till it finally finds rest in the Meeting-place of the waters, the great ocean far away. So, he says :— " A great kingdom, lowly like running water, is the Meeting-place of the world." Again, he says :—" Heavenly Love is like water. Water blesses all things, it does not hurt them." And again :—" The Rivers and Seas (because they seek a lowly place) are Lords of a hundred valleys. Let your love flow, seek a lowly place, and you will be Lord of a hundred valleys." He frequently returns, in his teaching, to the simile of water ; maintaining the fact that though it is the weakest, softest thing in nature, yet it has in it a force that can overcome that which is most strong.

Lao Tzŭ is essentially a prophet of peace, though he acknowledges the existence, perhaps even the necessity, of war. He deplores the occasion of war :—" He who has killed many men should weep with many tears." He insistently teaches that true progress is attainable only through the influence of Tao. " If you desire to gain the kingdom by action, I see that you will not succeed. The kingdom is a spiritual vessel, it cannot be gained by action." Yet true progress is not measured by man's standards, for " Brightness of Tao seems to be dark, Progress in Tao seems going back."

Many beautiful illustrations are given of the power of the self-controlled man who becomes the Man of Love. He learns to let his heart, his very thought, dwell in the Inner Kingdom ; and he draws the hearts of all men into his Heart. He blesses even the man who is not good ; he is faithful even to the man who is not faithful. He does not dwell apart from men ; but he patiently and persistently draws men into an active community of Heart—into that realm which some men, in these latter days, have named the supra-national Kingdom of Love. This Man of Love fears no danger, his Inner Life cannot be killed, it remains intact even when he passes into the place of Death.

It was natural that Lao Tzǔ should give his soldier-friend some teaching on government.

On this subject he says :—

" To govern a kingdom, use righteousness,

To conduct a war, use strategy,

To become a true world-ruler, be occupied with Inner Life."

This saying will stand the test of time and experience. It will prove its truth every time it is tested.

A curious chapter set in just before the last describes the condition of a kingdom shut in upon itself, as the " Middle Kingdom " really was until the war when Free Treaty Ports were forced upon the Chinese Nation. In this kingdom, which Lao Tzŭ describes so vividly, there is no give and take with other surrounding kingdoms. The people are innocent and happy, contented with small things, holding to ancient practices ; but having no outlets, no development nor growth.

The last chapter comes into sharp contrast with this condition of stagnation. It pictures the man who lives in Tao as one who is active, but not quarrelsome ; one who lives in order to give and to serve ; and who is ever thereby more and more enriched.

The *Tao Teh King* is written with a certain cadence. Groups of characters form phrases which often stand in paradox or contrast with the next group. It is impossible to translate this into English ; the bald single-word ideas must be linked together to convey their meaning to the mind of the modern non-Chinese reader. The translator has tried to bring out some of the cadence by setting the words of phrases on separate lines. The characters have usually been translated as literally as possible. Sometimes a translation is given which is not found in the dictionaries, but which seems to be the sum of the ideas indicated in the various component parts of the

character.   Throughout this translation the character wu 巫 has been rendered " Spirit in man,"
" Inner Life," or " innermost."   The translator
is conscious of many imperfections in the work,
but yet the translation is given in the hope that
others may be stimulated to search out for themselves the deep truths that lie hidden in this great
masterpiece of Lao Tzŭ.   The translations con-
sulted (but often not followed) are those of Mon-
sieur Stanislas Julien ; of Walter Gorn Old,
M.R.A.S. ; of Mr. Lionel Giles ; and of the late
Professor James Legge, to whom the translator
owes much gratitude.

PREFACE TO SECOND EDITION.

In sending out a second Edition of this translation
of Tao Teh King, some chapters have been re-set in
the hope of making the meaning more clear, and
some obvious mistakes have been corrected.

The translator thanks many friends, known and
unknown, for their words of kindly criticism and
appreciation.

BOOK I.

Called The Book of Tao

I.

THE Tao that can be expressed
　　is not Everlasting Tao.
The Name that can be named
　　is not the Everlasting Name.

He whose Name is " Spirit in Man "
　　is Life-spring of Heaven and Earth.
He whose Name is " outward possessions "
　　is Mother of all created beings.

Therefore constantly desire Inner Life
　　in order to perceive mysteries.
Constantly desire possessions
　　in order to perceive limitations.

These two : One in source but differing in Name
　　are One in being called deep,
　　Deep and yet more deep,
　　Door of many mysteries.

NOTE.—The first chapter of *Tao Teh King* may be
regarded as prologue of the book. In it the principles
of the Unseen and the Seen are clearly defined :　*Tao*,
Life, Source of Life ; and *Tao which can be named*, Mother
of all existing beings, later in the book named *Teh*, or
manifestation of Life ;—these are the two themes upon
which the book is built. The two are complimentary,
one is not praised at expense of the other, one cannot be
without the other ; in life we must take knowledge of
both.　To be busied with outer things, having no thought
of the inner, can only bring disaster.　To be busied with
Inner Life without regard to the Outer is impossible.

In seeking the Inner Life, we are more and more brought into the depths of its mystery. In seeking the outer, we are constantly brought up against its limitations. In seeking the Inner in and through the Outer, we find that the Source is One, we are led by degrees into deeper Mystery, into fuller realisation of Truth.

II.

ALL men know the existence of beauty.
Beauty, cleft asunder, is ugliness.

All men know the existence of love.
Love, cleft asunder, is hatred.

Therefore " possessions " and " Inner Life "
  interdepend in life.
Difficult and easy interdepend in completeness.
Long and short interdepend in form.
High and low interdepend in inequality.
Tones and voice interdepend in harmony.
Before and after interdepend in sequence.

That is why the self-controlled man
  makes it his business to dwell in the Inner Life ;
  he teaches, not by words, but by actions ;
  he brings all beings into action, he does not
    refuse them ;
  he gives them life, but does not possess them ;
  he acts, but looks not for reward ;
  he works out perfectness, but claims no credit.

The Master, indeed, rests not on rewards.
That is why he passes not away.

NOTE.—In the introduction to *British Destiny* Mr.
D. N. Dunlop gives a good commentary on the subject
of this chapter. He says:—" When man no longer
disregards the truths which a study of nature's laws
reveals, he will recognise the necessity for co-ordinating
all his affairs in conformity with these laws. He will
recognise the spiritual unity of the race at one pole,
and at the other his interdependence, as a physical
being, on other men."

NOTE on 聖 (self-controlled man).—This character
has usually been translated " sage " or " saint." It
is composed of three characters:—耳 (ear), 口 (mouth),
and 王 (a king). The idea in the character seems to
be " a man who controls what comes in to him by the
ear and what goes out from him by the mouth."

III.

EXALT not men,
  so that the people may not fight.
Prize not rare objects,
  so that the people may not steal.
Look not on desirable things,
  so that the people's heart be not troubled.

That is why the self-controlled man governs
        by stilling the emotions,
        by quieting thought,
        by mastering the will,
        by increasing strength.

    He always teaches the people
      to know the Inner Life,
      to desire the Inner Life.

  He teaches the Masters of knowledge
    to cease from activity,
    to act through activity of the Inner Life ;
    then Inner Life will govern all.

IV.

TAO is infinite.
If we use it, we find it inexhaustible.
Deep and unfathomable,
It seems to be Ancestor of all things.
It rounds off our angles,
It unravels our difficulties,
It tempers our light,
It is lowly as the dust,
It is pure,
It remains everlasting.
I do not know whose Son it is,
It appears to have existed before God.

V.

HEAVEN and earth are impartial,
   they regard all creatures as sacred.
The self-controlled man is impartial,
   he regards all people as sacred.

The space between Heaven and Earth is like
   a bellows.
   Emptied, it loses not power,
   Moved, it sends forth more and more wind.

   Many words lead to exhaustion.
   Be not thus ; keep to thy centre.

VI.

THE Spirit of the Valley dies not,
  it is called Mother-substance of the Deep.
The Door of Mother-substance of the Deep
  is called the Root of Heaven and Earth.

> Continuously, continuously,
> It nourishes and preserves.
> Use it,
> Thy strength shall not fail.

NOTE.—Lao Tzŭ frequently quotes from earlier sages or " sentence makers." This chapter is found in the works of Lieh Tse (400 B.C.). He quotes it from a book of the Emperor Hwang Ti (2700 B.C.). Lao Tzŭ here builds it into his system of philosophy.

VII.

HEAVEN and Earth endure long.

If Heaven and Earth endure long,
It is because they do not live for self,
Therefore they can long endure.

That is why the self-controlled man puts himself
  last,
Yet he is found in the foremost place.

He regards his body as outside of himself,
Yet his body is preserved.

Is it not that his chief interest is in the Inner Life ?
Therefore he can perfect his chief interest.

VIII.

HEAVENLY Love is like water.

Water blesses all things,
It does not hurt them.
It loves the lowly place that men dislike,
Therefore it comes very near to Tao.

The Master loves to dwell upon the earth.
In his heart he loves Infinity,
In his benevolence he loves giving,
In his words he loves sincerity,
In his government he loves peace,
In his business affairs he loves ability,
In his movements he loves punctuality.

The Master, indeed, does not fight,
Therefore his Inner Life increases.

IX.

LET Heavenly Love fill you and overflow in you,
Not according to your measure of fulness.

Prove it, probe deeply into it,
It shall not long withstand you.

You may fill a place with gold and precious stones,
You will not be able to guard them.

You may be weighted with honours and become
proud.
Misfortune then will come to your Self.

You may accomplish great deeds and acquire fame,
Retire yourself ;
This is Heavenly Tao.

X.

BRING soul and spirit into unity,
   they will become welded in the Inner Life.
Conquer vital force until it yields to you,
   you will become as a new-born child.
Purify the channels of deep perception,
   you will dwell safely in the Inner Life.
Govern a kingdom by governing the people,
   they will learn to act from the Inner Life.
Open and shut the doors of heaven,
   you will have repose of mind in active life.
Let your purity shine forth in all directions,
   men will see that you have the Inner Life.

   Give it birth, nourish it,
   Give it birth, but do not seek to possess.
   Act but do not appropriate.
   Endure but do not rule.
   This is called profound Teh.

XI.

THIRTY spokes surround one nave,
the usefulness of the wheel is always in that
empty innermost.

You fashion clay to make a bowl,
the usefulness of the bowl is always in that
empty innermost.

You cut out doors and windows to make a house,
their usefulness to a house is always in their
empty space.

Therefore profit comes from external form,
but usefulness comes from the empty innermost.

XII.

THE five colours blind the eyes of man.
The five musical notes deafen the ears of man.
The five flavours dull the taste of man.
Violent running and hunting disturb the emotions
of man.
Greed for rare objects is hurtful to the actions of
man.

That is why the self-controlled man occupies
himself with the unseen,
he does not occupy himself with the things
visible,
he puts away the latter and seeks the former.

NOTE.—The five colours are blue, red, yellow, black,
and white. The five notes of the Chinese musical scale
are G A B D E. The five flavours are salt, bitter, sour,
acid, and sweet.

XIII.

DREAD glory as you dread shame.
Prize great calamity as you prize your body.

What does this mean :
" Dread glory as you dread shame " ?
Glory comes from below.
Obtain it, you are afraid of shame ;
Lose it, you are still afraid of shame.
That is why it is said :
" Dread glory as you dread shame."

What does this mean :
" Prize great calamity as you prize your own
  body " ?
We who meet with great calamities,
  meet them because we have a body.
If we had not a body
  what calamity could reach us ?

Therefore he who honours the kingdom as his body
  can govern the kingdom.
He who loves the kingdom as his own body
  can be trusted with the kingdom.

XIV.

LOOKING at it, you do not see it,
   you call it Invisible.
Listening to it, you do not hear it,
   you call it Inaudible.
Touching it, you do not grasp it,
   you call it Intangible.
These three cannot be described,
   but they blend, and are One.

Above, it is not bright ;
Below, it is not dim ;
Unceasingly, unceasingly,
It cannot be called by a Name,
It enters into Form, and returns into Spirit.
That is why it is called Spiritual Form of Form,
   Spiritual Image of Image.
That is why it is called vague and indeterminate.
Meet it, you cannot see its beginning ;
Follow it, you cannot see its end.

Consider the Tao of Old
   in order to arrange affairs of Now.
To be able to know the Life-Spring of Old
   is to give expression to the Thread of the Tao.

NOTE.—The three qualities, Invisible, Inaudible,
and Intangible, " I, Hi, Wei," were considered by Jesuit

priests, and notably by M. Abel Rémusat (1823 A.D.), to be equivalent to the Hebrew "Jahve." That they have in them an attempt of the human mind to know and describe the unknowable is evidenced in the beautiful poem of Francis Thompson, which begins thus :—

> O world invisible, we view thee ;
> O world intangible, we touch thee ;
> O world unknowable, we know thee ;
> Inapprehensible, we clutch thee.

One could almost imagine that Francis Thompson had known and loved this chapter of Lao Tzŭ when he proceeds in the same poem to say :—

> But (when so sad thou canst not sadder)
> Cry ; and upon thy so sore loss
> Shall shine the traffic of Jacob's ladder
> Pitched betwixt Heaven and Charing Cross.

> Yea, in the night, my Soul, my daughter,
> Cry—clinging Heaven by the hems ;
> And lo, Christ walking on the water,
> Not of Genesareth, but Thames.

Truly, he considered well the " Tao of Old," and knew how to apply it to " affairs of Now."

XV.

Of old, those who were leaders in good actions
　　examined mysteries with deep penetration ;
　　searching deeply, they did not understand ;
　　even Masters did not understand ;
　　therefore their actions were void of strength.
They were timid, as those who cross a torrent in
　　　　winter ;
　　irresolute, as those who fear their neighbours ;
　　grave, as strangers before their host ;
　　they effaced themselves as ice that melts ;
　　they were rough as undressed wood,
　　empty as a valley,
　　confused as troubled water.

Who is able by quietness
　　to make pure the troubled heart ?
Who is able by repose
　　to become conscious of Inner Life ?

He who safely maintains his consciousness of Life
　　will find it to be inexhaustible ;
Even a Master will find it to be inexhaustible.
Therefore he will be able,
　　though not faultless,
　　to renew perfectness.

XVI.

To arrive at ultimate quietness
Steadfastly maintain repose.

All creatures together have form ;
I see them return again to their root.
The Master creatures come to perfect form,
Continuously they return to their root.
Continuous return to the root is called repose,
Repose is called the law of return,
The law of return is called eternity.
To know eternity is called illumination,
To ignore eternity is to draw misfortune on oneself,
To know eternity is to be great of Soul,
To be great of soul is to be a ruler,
To be a ruler is to be greater than all,
To be greater than all is to be conscious of Life,
To be conscious of Life is to endure.
The body shall disappear but not decay.

XVII.

IN ancient times
The people knew that they had rulers.
Then they loved and praised them,
Then they feared them,
Then they despised them.

The rulers did not trust the people,
The people did not trust the rulers.

The rulers were grave, their words were precious.
The people having finished their work,
    and brought it to a successful issue, said :—
      " We are sufficient in ourselves."

XVIII.

GREAT Tao lost,
There came duty to man and right conduct.

Wisdom and shrewdness appearing,
There came great hypocrisy.

The six relationships inharmonious,
There came filial piety deep, deep in the heart.

Kingdoms, families, and clans at war,
There came loyal Ministers.

NOTE.—The " six relationships " are those of father
and son, elder brother and younger brother, husband
and wife.

XIX.

IF the people renounce self-control and reject
   wisdom,
Let them gain simplicity and purity.

If the people renounce duty to man and reject
   right conduct,
Let them return to filial piety deep, deep in the
   heart.

If they renounce skill and leave off search for
   profit,
Let them rob and by violence take possession of
   spiritual life.

These three things do not help our progress.
Therefore now let us seek
To perceive simplicity,
To conserve beauty in the heart,
To curb selfishness and to have few desires.

XX.

RENOUNCE learning, it brings loss to the Inner Life.

How slight the difference between Yes and Yea !
How great the difference between Good and Evil !
That which men fear is indeed to be feared.
When men give themselves up to disorder it never
  stops.

Many men rejoice and rejoice
  over a supply of good food,
  over being in a high and exalted position.
I am calm, I do not feel the slightest emotion,
  like a new-born child which cannot yet smile
    at its mother,
  without attachment to anything,
  returning always to the Inner Life.

Many men have superfluous possessions.
I have nothing that I value ;
  I desire that my heart be completely subdued,
  emptied to emptiness.

Men of wealth are in the daylight of prosperity.
I am in the dark.

Men of wealth are endowed with penetration.
I appear confused and ignorant.
  Suddenly I am, as it were, on a vast sea,
  floating on the sea of Inner Life which is bound-
    less.

Many men are full of ability.
I appear to be stupid and rustic.

Thus am I different from other men.
But I revere the Mother, Sustainer of all beings.

NOTE.—A brief commentary on this chapter is found
in the words of St. Paul :—" I count *all things* but loss
. . . that I may win Christ, and be found in Him " ;
for the Inner Life is the Christ Life, and none else. Again
the mystic poet Francis Thompson, in " The Mistress
of Vision," says :—

> Pierce thy heart to find the key ;
>
> .   .   .   .
>
> When thy seeing blindeth thee
> To what thy fellow-mortals see ;
> When their sight to thee is sightless ;
> Their living, death ; their light, most lightless ;
> Search no more—
> Pass the gates of Luthany, tread the region Elenore.

It is most true that those who dare to pierce their heart
to find the key find also that they have gained entrance
to the land of Harmony, to the region where God speaks
inwardly ; where they have new eyes, new values of life,
new measurements of gain and loss.

XXI.

THE complete manifestation of things visible
    proceeds only from Life.

In its nature Life is always coming into activity,
    yet in itself it eludes our sight and touch.

Eluding sight ! eluding touch !
Within it are hid the plans of created things.
Eluding touch ! eluding sight !
Within it are hid all created beings.

It is profound ! It is obscure !
Within it is hid pure Spirit.
It is pure Spirit, enfolding Truth !
Within it is hid an infallible witness.

From of Old until Now
Its Name remains unchanged.
Through its Doorway comes the Universe into
    existence.

How do I know that
    the Universe is coming to full perfection through
        Life ?
The witness is in Life itself.

NOTE.—At the beginning of our study of the *Tao
Teh King* we found, by analysis of the characters, that

the meaning of *Tao* seemed to be Progressive Intelligence or Life-Consciousness; and *Teh*, Manifestation of Life. As we proceed with the study, giving attention now to the dominant idea of the book, we seem to find that the only adequate English equivalent for *Tao* is *Life*. The Tao is magical Master of change, giving a mysterious urge to the expression of Itself in form, to growth towards maturity, to continuous evolution leading to perfectness, to such a fulness of Life that " decay " is precluded. Transmutation, transfusion, and transformation are all in the scheme of Tao as in the scheme of Life; they overcome decay as Life overcomes death. So, in another small book dealing with Life, the Gospel of St. John, we read of Life finding expression in the Word, " making " all things, giving light of understanding to men, giving power to those who receive of its fulness. We read of One so full of Life that it was easy for Him to transmute elements, to transfuse health into those who lacked it, to transform men from a low moral grade to a high spiritual grade. We read that this same One had such fulness of Life in Himself that when He was crucified and " dead " His mortal body did not decay, but was transmuted into a spiritual body which burst the bonds of death, came out of the grave, and gave assurance of a boundless and inexhaustible well of Life for men. In relation to this chapter it is interesting to note the following quotations from the *Bhagavad Gita* :—

> Ch. xi., v. 15—" Within Thy Form, O God, the Gods I see,
> All grades of beings with distinctive marks."
> Ch. xi., v. 31—" Thine inner being I am fain to know ;
> This Thy forthstreaming Life bewilders me."

XXII.

THAT which is incomplete becomes complete.

> The crooked becomes straight,
> The empty becomes full,
> The worn-out becomes new.

> He who obtains has little,
> He who scatters has much.

That is why the self-controlled man holds to
　Unity and brings it into manifestation for men.
He looks not at self, therefore he sees clearly ;
He asserts not himself, therefore he shines ;
He boasts not of self, therefore he has merit ;
He glorifies not himself, therefore he endures.

The Master indeed does not strive,
　yet no one in the world can strive against him.

The words of the Ancients were not empty words :
" That which is incomplete becomes complete."

> Acquire completeness by returning it.

XXIII.

WITH few words affirm thyself.

A great wind does not blow all the morning,
A heavy rain does not continue all day.
Why is it so ?
It is because of the inter-relations of Heaven
  and Earth.

If Heaven and Earth cannot make things last long,
How much less can man !

Therefore he who follows the service of Tao
  is one with Tao,
He who is virtuous is one with Teh,
He who fails is one with failure.

He who is one with Tao,
Tao shall also claim him.
He who is one with Teh,
Teh shall also claim him.
He who is one with failure,
Failure shall also claim him.
Faith that is not complete is not faith.

NOTE.—To " affirm self " seems to mean that we
should not be concerned with negatives nor with failures ;
but that we should live in the affirmative aspect of life,
reaching always out after goodness, and letting our personal influence flow out in blessing, without effort. The
phrase recurs in later chapters.

XXIV.

He who stands on tiptoe is not steady,
He who holds the legs stiffly cannot walk.

He who looks at self does not see clearly.
He who asserts himself does not shine.
He who boasts of himself has no merit.
He who glorifies himself shall not endure.

These things are to the Tao
  like excreta or a hideous tumour to the body.
Therefore he who has the Tao
  must give them no place.

XXV.

THERE was a Being already perfect
  before the existence of Heaven and Earth.
It is calm ! It is formless !
It stands alone and changes not !
Reaching everywhere and inexhaustible,
It may be regarded as Mother of the Universe.

I do not know its name.
For a title we call it the Tao.
If forced to give it a name we call it the Great.
Great, we call it the Flowing,
Flowing, we call it distant,
Distant, we call it the Coming again.

Therefore the Tao is Great, Heaven is Great,
The Earth is Great, the Ruler also is Great.
In the Universe four are Great,
And the Ruler is one of them.

Man finds his law in the Earth.
The Earth finds its law in Heaven,
Heaven finds its law in the Tao,
The Tao finds its law in the affirmation of Itself.

NOTE.—Compare :—
  First of the Gods, most ancient Man Thou art,
  Supreme receptacle of all that lives ;
  Knower and known, the dwelling-place on high ;
  In Thy vast Form the Universe is spread.
            —*Bhagavad Gita*, xi. 38.

XXVI.

GRAVITY is the root of lightness,
Quiescence is the master of motion.

That is why a king's son
   though he may travel all day long,
   does not cease to be quiet and grave ;
   though he may achieve glory
   he abides in restfulness,
   he affirms his detachment.

How sad it would be
   if the Lord of a thousand chariots
   should conduct himself lightly in the kingdom !

If his conduct is light, he will fail as a Minister ;
If he is hasty in action, he will fail as a Ruler.

XXVII.

He who walks in goodness leaves his trace in the
Inner Life.
He who speaks in goodness carries no blame to
the Inner Life.
He who reckons in goodness does not need to
use a tally.

The good man has power to close the inner door
and no one can open it.
The good man has power to tie the inner knot
and no one can untie it.

That is why the self-controlled man
always uses goodness in helping men,
thus he draws them to the Inner Life.
He always uses goodness in helping creatures,
thus he draws them to the Inner Life.
This is called being doubly illuminated.

Therefore the good man masters the man who
is not good,
And the man who is not good is helper to the
good man.

He who does not honour his master,
He who does not love his helper,
Though counted wise, is greatly deceived.
This is called important and mysterious.

XXVIII.

To know manly strength, to guard womanly
  gentleness,
Is to be the central channel of the kingdom.
To be the central channel of the kingdom,
  always manifesting life, never guilty,
  is to return to the innocence of childhood.

To know light, to guard the darkness,
Is to be the model of the kingdom.
To be the model of the kingdom
  always manifesting life, never at fault,
  is to return to the bounds of the Inner Kingdom.

To know glory, to guard humility,
Is to be the valley of the kingdom.
To be the valley of the kingdom,
  always manifesting life, becoming perfect,
  is to return to a condition like undressed wood.

Undressed wood, being made into many utensils,
The self-controlled man uses them,
Then he becomes Ruler for a long time.
Thus he achieves greatness without hurt to
  anyone.

XXIX.

IF you desire to gain the kingdom by action,
I see that you will not succeed.
The kingdom is a spiritual vessel,
It cannot be gained by action.
He who acts, destroys it.
He who grasps, loses it.

Therefore behold the animals :
   Some go in front, others follow ;
   Some are warm, others are cold ;
   Some are strong, others are feeble ;
   Some keep moving, others are still.

That is why the self-controlled man
   puts away excess,
   he puts away egotism,
   he puts away easy living.

NOTE.—The argument seems to be that we do not conquer environment by action but by intuition, as animals do by instinct ; but that man, seeking higher things, must further practise renunciation. Compare the teaching of Edward Carpenter in " Have Faith " :—
" Absolve yourself to-day from the bonds of action."
. . . " Begin to-day to understand why the animals are not hurried, and do not concern themselves about affairs, nor the clouds nor the trees nor the stars—but only man—and he but for a few thousand years in history."
. . . " Give away all that you have, become poor and without possessions—and behold ! you shall be lord and sovereign of all things."

XXX.

He who would help a Ruler of men by Tao
Does not take soldiers to give strength to the
  kingdom.
His service is well rewarded.

Where troops dwell, there grow thorns and briers.
After great wars, there follow bad years.

He who loves, bears fruit unceasingly,
He does not dare to conquer by strength.
He bears fruit, but not with assertiveness,
He bears fruit, but not with boastfulness,
He bears fruit, but not with meanness,
He bears fruit, but not to obtain it for himself,
He bears fruit, but not to shew his strength.

Man is great and strong, then he is old,
In this he is not of Tao.
If he is not of Tao
He quickly will perish.

XXXI.

THE Master who is a Captain of soldiers
Does not give blessings with his weapons.
Soldiers' weapons are hated by most men,
Therefore he who has the Tao gives them no place.

In the dwelling of the man of peace
   the left side is the place of honour.
In soldiers' usage
   the right side is the place of honour.

A soldier does not give blessings with his weapons.
They are not the instruments of a man of peace.
A man of peace will not possess them, nor use them;
He gives the first place to calmness and repose.

If he conquers, he does not rejoice.
Without joy is he who wounds and kills men.
The Master who wounds and kills men
Cannot succeed in ruling his kingdom.

In time of joy, the left hand is preferred,
In time of mourning, the right hand is preferred.
In war, the second in command is placed on the
   left,
The first in command is placed on the right,
That is, he stands in the place of mourning.

He who has killed many men
   should weep with many tears.
He who has conquered in battle
   should stand in the place of mourning.

NOTE.—The Duke of Wellington echoed the sentiment of sorrow for the slain when he said :—" To gain a battle is the saddest thing next to losing it."   With regard to the " place of honour," Julien says :—" The left side refers to the principle of activity, it is the symbol of life ; in happy events (as in marriages) the left hand is the place of honour.   The right side refers to the principle of inertia, it is the symbol of death ; in mournful events (as in funeral rites) the right hand is the place of honour."

XXXII.

THE Name of Inner Life is Everlasting Tao.

If only he is pure, though he may be small,
The Servant of Tao dares to stand against the
    world.

Tao is able to maintain the unity of prince and
    people ;
It subdues and binds all beings with each other ;
It unites Heaven and Earth harmoniously to
    produce the sweet dew ;
It gathers the people in the bonds of time and
    individuality.

The Name produces, divides, and brings to life ;
Things produced ever return into the Name.

The Master also shall know how to rest in it.
Knowing how to rest in it means that he never
    will decay.

On the earth everywhere Tao exists,
As the waters are collected in the valleys
And return into the rivers and the seas.

XXXIII.

HE who knows men is wise,
He who knows himself can see clearly.

He who conquers men has strength,
He who conquers himself has power.

He who knows that he has enough is rich,
He who acts with energy has a strong will.

He who fails not to find the Self shall endure,
He who dies, but does not perish, shall endure
   for ever.

NOTE.—Prof. Legge, in his Note on this chapter,
says that the Indian monk Kumaragiva, " one of the four
suns of Buddhism," who went to China A.D. 401, com-
mented thus :—" To be alive and yet not alive may well
be called long ; to die and yet not be dead may well be
called longevity." He also gives the views of Lu Nang-
shih (A.D. 1042-1102) that the human body is like the
covering of the caterpillar or the skin of the snake ; that
we occupy it but for a passing sojourn.

XXXIV.

GREAT Tao flows everywhere,
It extends to the left and to the right.

All beings receive It
  in order to live and to be free.
It works out perfectness in them
  although It possesses not a Name.

It protects them with love and sustains them,
  but does not claim to be Ruler of their actions.
Always seeking the innermost,
  you may say that Its Name is in the Small.

All beings return again into It,
  yet It does not claim to be Ruler of their actions.
You may say that Its Name is in the Great.

That is why, to the end of his life,
  the self-controlled man is not great in action,
Thus he is able to perfect his greatness.

NOTE.—The "flow of Great Tao" seems to find a parallel in the philosophy of Henri Bergson, as set forth in H. Wildon Carr's book, "The Philosophy of Change." "Reality is not solid matter, nor thinking mind, but living creative evolution. It seems as if a great movement were in progress, sweeping us along in the living stream, as it were on the breast of a wave. The actual present now in which all existence is gathered up is this movement accomplishing itself. The past is gathered into it, exists in it, is carried along in it, as it presses forward into the future, which is continually and without intermission becoming actual. This reality is life. It is an unceasing becoming, which preserves the past and creates the future."

XXXV.

HOLD fast the idea of " The Great,"
Then all men will be drawn to you.
They will come to you and receive no hurt,
But rest, peace and great calm.

When you provide music and exquisite food
The traveller will stay with you gladly.
When the Tao flows out from you to him
By his palate he does not detect its savour,
By his eyes he cannot perceive it,
By his ears he cannot hear it,
But in using it he finds it to be inexhaustible.

XXXVI.

IF you desire to breathe deeply,
   you must first empty the lungs.
If you desire to be strong,
   you must first learn to be weak.
If you desire to be in a lofty position,
   you must first learn to take a lowly position.
If you desire to be enriched by gifts,
   you must first give away all that you have.
This is called concealment and enlightenment.

The soft overcomes the hard.
The weak overcomes the strong.
Fish cannot swim safely in shallow waters.
The secrets of government of a kingdom
   should not be revealed to the people.

NOTE.—This chapter, along with others in the book, teaches the principle of Alternation, Pulsation, Rhythm. The heart must be emptied before it can be filled with vital fluid, in order to fulfil its function. The lung-cells must be emptied of vitiated air before they can vitalise the body by the inflow of vital air. A muscle must be relaxed, made apparently quite weak, before it can manifest its fulness of action. So, the Sage tells us, in the moral world we must learn to take a lowly place if we would be great. Above all, we must learn to give most freely if we desire to be enriched by true riches. It is only by means of Alternation that function can be perfectly performed. A muscle always slack is useless ; a muscle always tense is worse than useless ; it is only by the alternation of weakness and strength that strength can be brought into usefulness. There is a wonderful depth of truth in this principle. By the conscious practice of alternation we may attain to greater perfectness in the activities of daily life, whether these be physical, moral or spiritual. Alternation means reiteration, returning. Therefore, " he who returns is sent forth by Tao " ; he who has the secret of return from outward activity to the Source of Life shall be renewed in strength, in proportion as he avails himself of this principle.

XXXVII.

THE activity of Everlasting Tao is in the Inner
  Kingdom,
It does not act except through the innermost.

If prince and people can maintain it together,
All beings will be transformed from within them-
  selves ;
Being transformed, they again desire action.

We must learn to still desire
To obtain in the Inner Life Purity of the Name.

Purity of the Name in the Inner Life
Brings absence of desire ;
Absence of desire brings stillness ;
Thus shall the world be perfected from within
    itself.

NOTE.—A beautiful parallel passage, dealing with
the activity of Everlasting Life in the Inner Kingdom,
is found in the words of Edith Christison (" New-England
Tragedies," by Longfellow) :—

> Truly, we do but grope here in the dark,
> Near the partition-wall of Life and Death,
> At every moment dreading or desiring
> To lay our hands upon the unseen door !
> Let us, then, labour for an inward stillness—
> An inward stillness and an inward healing ;
> That perfect silence where the lips and heart
> Are still, and we no longer entertain
> Our own imperfect thoughts and vain opinions,
> But God alone speaks in us, and we wait
> In singleness of heart, that we may know
> His will, and in the silence of our spirits,
> That we may do His will, and do that only !

BOOK II.

Called The Book of Teh

XXXVIII.

To assume virtue without being really virtuous
  is to be virtuous from duty ;
To be less virtuous, yet not to lose real virtue,
  is to be virtuous from Inner Life.

Supreme virtue comes through activity of Inner
    Life ;
  then let us actively seek Inner Life.
To be less virtuous and to practise it,
  let us be active in the performance of duty.

To assume benevolence and practise it
  let us actively seek Inner Life.
To assume right conduct and practise it
  let us be active in the performance of duty.
To assume expediency and practise it is to find
    that no one honours it ;
  then it bares the arm, and asserts itself by force.

Therefore, when Tao is lost, follow Virtue ;
  when virtue is lost, follow benevolence ;
  when benevolence is lost, follow right conduct ;
  when right conduct is lost, follow expediency.

Those who are Masters of expediency
  have in the heart only the shadow of faith,
  and in the mind only confusion.

Those who are Leaders of politeness
  have only the husk of Tao,
  which is the source of ignorance.

That is why the greatest of the Masters
  abide in the real,
  they do not abide in the shadow.
They hold to the fruit,
  they do not hold to the husk.
Therefore they put away the latter
  and take hold of the former.

NOTE on Teh, or Virtue.—The English word " virtue "
is limited, cold, and colourless compared to the idea
underlying Teh ; yet it seems as if no other single word
can be found to render it. In Teh is the idea of the
realisation and manifestation of Life. It is Tao made
manifest. It is, as it were, the systole of the great Heart
of Life, while Tao is the diastole. Teh is the multiplicity
of which Tao is the Unity. Its roots are therefore in
Tao, and without Tao it cannot exist. It is the com-
plement of the Infinite, the revelation of Divinity. It is
Nature, in and through which God is revealed ; it is
His Goodness, Wisdom and Beauty incarnate. Lao
Tzŭ's idea in this chapter seems to be that of old Teh
was realised and sought after, but that man forsook its
Way and followed a down-grade through the steps of
benevolence ; right conduct ; expediency, which led to
war ; and politeness or ceremonial, which is the mere
husk of Teh. Therefore his counsel is " Get back into
Teh, find the real, leave the shadow."

XXXIX.

THESE are they which from of Old have obtained
Unity.
  Heaven obtained Unity by purity ;
  The earth obtained Unity by repose;
  Spiritual beings obtained Unity by lack of
    bodily form ;
  The valleys obtained Unity by fulness ;
  All beings obtained Unity by life ;
  Princes and people obtained Unity by being
    under the rule of Heaven.
  These all obtained permanence by Unity.

The innermost of Heaven is purity,
  if not so, it would be obscured ;
The innermost of Earth is repose,
  if not so, it would disintegrate ;
The innermost of spiritual beings is lack of bodily
    form,
  if not so, they would die ;
The innermost of valleys is fulness of water,
  if not so, they would be sterile ;
The innermost of creatures is life,
  if not so, they would perish.
The high honour of prince and people
  is in their being together under the rule of
    Inner Life,
  if not so, they would soon lose harmony.

The root of honour is in humility,
The standpoint of high estate is in lowliness.

That is why prince and people call themselves
    orphans,
  solitary men, chariots without wheels.
The active principle of their Unity is in lowliness.
Who can deny this?
If you take a chariot to pieces,
  you have no chariot (it has lost its Unity).
Do not desire to be isolated as a single gem,
    nor to be lost in a crowd as pebbles on the
      beach.

XL.

HE who returns is sent forth by Tao,
He who is weak is used by Tao.

In the world things are born into existence,
Existing things are born into Inner Life.

NOTE.—This short chapter tells of Tao informing
Teh; of Inner Life expressing Itself through outward
form; of Force using weakness; of Life made manifest
in existence; of existing things being "born again,"
and henceforward holding the jewel of Life in the innermost of their being.

XLI.

WHEN great scholars heard of Tao,
  they diligently followed it.
When mediocre scholars heard of Tao,
  sometimes they kept it, sometimes they lost it.
When inferior scholars heard of Tao,
  they laughed at it.
Whether they laugh or whether they follow,
  Tao remains active.

Therefore the poets have said :—
  Brightness of Tao seems to be dark,
  Progress in Tao seems going back,
  The aim of Tao seems confused.
  The highest Teh seems lowliest,
  Great purity seems full of shame,
  The fullest Teh seems incomplete.
  Teachers of Teh have lost their zeal
  And certain Truth appears to change.
  A great square with inner angles,
  A great vase unfinished,
  A great voice never heard,
  A great Image with inner form.

Tao is hid within its Name,
But by Tao the Masters bless,
And all things bring to perfectness.

XLII.

In Tao is Unity of Life,
In Unity is Duality of Life,
In Duality is Trinity of Life,
In Trinity all beings have Life.

All beings shun the principle of Inertia,
They hold to the principle of Life.
They are brought into harmony by the Breath
of the Deep.

That which men dislike
is to be called orphans, solitary, wheels without
naves ;
Yet princes and rulers may thus be named.

Therefore some are increased by being diminished,
And some are diminished by being increased.

That which men have taught
I also shall teach :
" He who is strong and violent shall not meet
with easy death."
I shall in this way teach fundamentals.

Note on Unity.—In Tao is Unity of Life ; from Tao
comes Manifestation in Form, or Duality of Life ; but

Duality cannot exist without a third quality, " touch,"
which brings rhythm, poise, balance, perfect adjustment
of the Two.   All beings have, in themselves, a Trinity of
Life, Form and Function.   Thus Trinity of being reverts
into indissoluble Unity.   We meet with Duality of Life
on every hand—Good and Evil, Love and Hate, Beauty
and Ugliness, Light and Darkness, Pleasure and Pain,
Joy and Sorrow, and many others.   We say that these
are opposites.   In our view the presence of the one
seems to preclude the presence of the other.   We say
that each of them exists but that they do not co-exist.
Yet if we follow the thought of Lao Tzŭ (see Ch. II.)
we find that they interdepend ; that they can be harmonised by the Breath of the Deep ; that they are, in
fact, parts of a perfect Whole.   Our trouble comes from
thinking of them as being separate—different in essence,
one to be shunned and the other to be sought after—
and from not realising that they are as essential to each
other as the positive and negative poles of a battery,
which are brought into usefulness of function by " touch."
Many people find, by experience, that Good and Evil
are interchangeable :—

> " Ill that God blesses is our good,
>   And unblest good is ill."—*Faber*.

Further, we find that Love, the Breath of Love out of
the Deeps of God, the wonderful solvent, the " touch "
that brings usefulness of function, can and does constantly transpose and transform evil into good, sorrow
into joy, ugliness into beauty.   Therefore, though at
the end of this chapter we have a note on the finality of
karma, yet we believe that Love covers Sin, and that,
" come what can or will, Love makes amends for all."
Let us, then, more diligently apply the unitive touch of
Love.

XLIII.

In the world when we arrive at gentleness we
press forward to overcome all hardness.

To possess Inner Life
we enter it by our own private doorway.

We do this in order to know in overflowing fulness
the possession of activity of Inner Life.

Overflowing fulness of activity of Inner Life
With power to impart it to others without words—
Few men in the world attain to this.

Note.—By our own doorway we come into our
earthly life, and by our own doorway we leave our earthly
life. So, the Sage tells us, by our own doorway we enter
into consciousness of our inner, spiritual life. We cannot
enter by another man's door, only by our own individual,
private door. Each one who thus enters into the conscious
possession of his spiritual life begins at once to realise
that it is superabundant, overflowing, ever freshly
springing up. It puts fresh impulse into everything we
may do or say. It flows out from us to others in a living
stream of love, often unconsciously to ourselves, often
consciously, but always fruitfully. So we keep on sending
to others, spending for others, giving to others, blessing
others, in exact proportion as we open our doorway to
let the love and blessing come through from the Great
Fountain of all love and all blessing.

XLIV.

WHICH is more dear to you,
  Your character or your body?

Which do you treasure more,
  your body or your wealth?

Which makes you more unhappy,
  to gain or to lose?

But we must sacrifice much to gain true love.
We must suffer great loss to obtain much treasure.

To know contentment is to fear no shame.
To know how to stop is to avoid destruction.
Thus doing, we shall long endure.

XLV.

ESTEEM lightly your greatest accomplishment,
  your patience will not fail.
Reckon your great fulness to be emptiness,
  your strength will not become exhausted.
Count your rectitude as foolishness,
Know your cleverness to be stupidity,
Recognise your eloquence to be stammering words,
And you will find that
As movement overcomes cold,
  and as stillness overcomes heat,
    even so, he who knows the true secret of tran-
    quillity
Will become a pattern for all mankind.

XLVI.

When Tao was manifested to men,
Horses were used for cultivating the fields.

When Tao was hid within Itself,
War horses were reared on the frontiers.

There is no sin greater than desire,
There is no misfortune greater than discontent,
There is no calamity greater than the wish to
   acquire,
Therefore to be satisfied is an everlasting
   sufficiency.

XLVII.

Without going out of my door
   I know the Universe.

Without opening my window
   I perceive Heavenly Tao.

The more I go abroad, the less I understand.

That is why the self-controlled man
   arrives without going,
   names things without seeing them,
   perfects without activity.

XLVIII.

By activity in learning we are daily enriched.
By activity of Tao we are daily diminished,
  diminished and yet more diminished,
  until we arrive at activity of Inner Life,
  and activity of Inner Life becomes stillness
    of Inner Life.

By the practice of Inner Life stillness
  we can continually conquer all things.
By the practice of returning to possessions,
  nothing that we conquer will be sufficient
    for us.

NOTE.—An illustration of activity in stillness is
in the spinning of a top. At its greatest speed there is
most apparent stillness, and we say that the top is then
" asleep."

In reading this chapter one is reminded of Words-
worth's " wise passiveness " on the " old grey stone " :—

> I deem that there are Powers
>   Which of themselves our minds impress,
> That we can feed this mind of ours
>   In a wise passiveness.
>
> Think you, 'mid all this mighty sum
>   Of things for ever speaking,
> That nothing of itself will come,
>   But we must still be seeking ?
>
> Then ask not wherefore, here, alone,
>   Conversing as I may,
> I sit upon this old grey stone
>   And dream my time away.

These well-known lines take us usefully to Francis Thompson's *Contemplation* :—

> No hill can idler be than I,
> No stone its inter-particled vibration
> Investeth with a stiller lie ;
> No heaven with a more urgent rest betrays
> The eyes that on it gaze.
> We are too near akin that thou shouldst cheat
> Me, Nature, with thy fair deceit.
> In poets floating like a water-flower
> Upon the bosom of the glassy hour,
> In skies that no man sees to move,
> Lurk untumultuous vortices of power,
> For joy too native, and for agitation
> Too instant, too entire for sense thereof—
> Motion like gnats when summer suns are low,
> Perpetual as the prisoned feet of love
> On the heart's floors with pained pace that go.
> From stones and poets you may know
> Nothing so active is as that which least seems so.

Thus do the Tao, the top, the stone, and the poet explain one another.

I should like, however, to call two other witnesses, twins in science, which give picturesque and suggestive evidence. Even as there are two sorts of inactivity—the sub-activity, which is true inactivity, and the super-activity of Tao, top, stone, and poet, which is only apparent inactivity—so there are two kinds of silence and two kinds of darkness. Of the gamut of sound vibrations only one portion is sensed by our human ears. The part below is silence to us, and the part above is silence. But the nether silence and the upper silence are not the same silence, for the former is the indolence of sound waves, or their complete passivity, and the silence above is sound whose "unperturbed velocity the spirit of the simoon mocks," and for which we may find no hospitable ear. Passing from these comparatively coarse vibrations in the ruder medium of the air to the nobler, more subtle, vibrations of the ether, we find a parallel. Only a very restricted area of the long scale of ether vibrations is visible to our normal physical eyes. That region is but an octave ; each note of it is a colour ; and when all are played together there comes crystal light. It is as if we had pianos, and all other musical instruments, of only one, and the same, octave. Exquisite work is done by nature and by man on that brief island of light. But what would be achieved if we had at our disposal as many of the octaves of light as we have of sound ? To such an evolution of our physical sight, if the *élan vital* should not choose a better route, we look forward. Meanwhile beneath our delectable little octave of colours is darkness, a thing less active, less subtle, than itself, or, indeed, wholly passive, while above it, too, is darkness, but darkness more active, more subtle, than itself—darkness that is as the stillness of the Tao, the top, the stone, and the poet, which explain one another—and Nirvana, and Brahma, and God.—C. R. W. F.

XLIX.

THE Heart of the self-controlled man
  is always in the Inner Kingdom.
He draws the hearts of all men into his Heart.

If a man is good, he blesses him ;
If a man is not good, still he blesses him with the
  Blessing of Teh.
If a man is faithful, he is faithful to him ;
If a man is not faithful, still he is faithful to him
  with the Faithfulness of Teh.

The self-controlled man dwells in the world.
Patiently and persistently
He brings the whole world into active community
  of Heart.

All men turn their ears and their eyes towards him.
They are all the children of the self-controlled man.

NOTE on " Heart."—Devendranath Tagore gives
forth the idea of blessing mankind through Heart-work
in the words :—" Now I have come to know that great
Sun-coloured Being beyond the darkness . . . . . .
Henceforward I shall radiate light from my heart upon
the world ; for I have reached the Sun, and darkness
has vanished."

L.

WE come into Life, we enter Death.

Three out of ten men follow the way of Life.
Three out of ten men follow the way of Death.
Also there are three out of ten who live as men
   and yet they move on to the place of Death.

What a Master is he, therefore,
   who takes hold of Life, of real Life!
He lives, his ears open to goodness,
   listening to hidden things.

In travelling, he fears not the rhinoceros nor tiger.
In entering the war-chariot, he dreads not the
   weapon of the soldier.
Can a rhinoceros with his horn strike the Inner
   Life?
Can a tiger with his claw tear the Inner Life?
Can a soldier with his weapon pierce the valley
   of Inner Life?

What a Master is he, therefore,
   who into the place of Death
   can bring his Inner Life!

   NOTE.—Compare :—

   I say to thee weapons reach not the Life ;
   Flame burns it not, waters cannot o'erwhelm,
   Nor dry winds wither it.
                            —*The Song Celestial*, Book II.

LI.

TAO gives Life to all beings.
Teh nourishes them.
It gives to each being its form,
It gives the inward urge towards perfectness.

That is why there is no living creature
  that does not reverence Tao
  and honour Teh.

The veneration of Tao !
The honour of Teh !
No Master has decreed it,
But eternally it is self-affirmed !

Therefore Tao gives Life to all beings,
It nourishes and makes them grow,
It rears them and perfects them,
It sustains, feeds, and protects them.

It gives them Life, but does not possess them.
It gives them activity, but does not depend on
  them.
It urges them to grow, but does not rule them.
This is called profound Teh.

LII.

WHILE in the world gain possession of the Life-
Spring
in order that you may become a World-Mother.

When you have attained to Motherhood
you will know your children.
When you know your children
you will retain your Motherhood.
Then, though the body may disappear,
You will not be hurt.

Close the door of the mouth,
Shut the doors of the senses,
Throughout life your body will not be fatigued.

Open the mouth,
Increase your business affairs,
Throughout life your body will not be safe.

To perceive the small is called clear vision.
To guard the weak is called strength.

Follow the Light, you will reflect its radiance.
Neglect the Inner Life, your body will meet with
calamity.
This is called the eternal heritage.

LIII.

IF I have knowledge and resolute faith
I shall walk in the Great Tao.
If I fear,
I can only behave well outwardly.

Great Tao is very straight,
But the people love by-roads.

The palace may be well kept,
But the fields may be uncultivated
And the granaries empty.

The Princes take more land,
At their girdle they carry a sword,
They eat dainty food,
They take possession of much gold.

This is called glorification of robbery.
It is not Tao.

NOTE.—Compare :—

My son, trust not in your present wishes,
They will soon change.
You will be slave of life-long fickleness,
Though you wish it not.

.   .   .   .

But high above these things that change is the wise
    man with spirit well taught,
Who cares not what he feels,
Nor from what quarter blows the shifting breeze,
If but the holy motive of his mind go onward to the
    due and longed-for end.
For thus will he be able to remain the same, unshaken,
Pointing the simple eye of motive
Through many changing chances straight at Me.
The purer that this eye of motive is
The straighter sails the vessel through the many
    storms.

—Thomas a Kempis.

LIV.

HE who is established in goodness
  shall not be uprooted.
He who cherishes goodness
  shall not be cast out.
His children to all generations
  shall be blessed unceasingly.

Cultivate it in the body,
  your Teh shall become true.
Cultivate it in the family,
  your Teh shall superabound.
Cultivate it in the village,
  your Teh shall endure.
Cultivate it in the kingdom,
  your Teh shall flourish.
Cultivate it in the world,
  your Teh shall be universal.

Therefore, according to the body, judge the body.
According to the family, judge the family.
According to the village, judge the village.
According to the kingdom, judge the kingdom.
According to the world, judge the world.

How shall I know that there is some faith in the
  world?
The witness is in itself.

LV.

HE who has his foundation in Teh
　is like a little child.

Poisonous insects do not sting him,
Wild beasts do not seize him,
Birds of prey do not strike at him.

His bones are weak, his muscles soft,
Yet he can take hold firmly.

He is ignorant of sex, but is full of vitality.
He will grow to maturity.

All day long he shouts and sings.
He will arrive at a knowledge of harmony.

The knowledge of harmony is called eternal.
The knowledge of eternal things is called clear
　vision.

Increase of life does not always bring happiness.
The life-force that gives birth to human emotion
　is strong.
Human emotion comes to full power and then
　grows old.

It is not Tao.
If it is not Tao, it quickly will perish.

LVI.

HE who knows, speaks not ;
He who speaks, knows not.

He closes the mouth,
He shuts the doors of the senses.
He subdues activities,
He is freed from bonds.
He diffuses Light,
He gathers men into Unity.
This is called wonderful Unity.

Favour and disgrace do not touch him,
Profit and loss do not affect him,
Honour and shame are alike to him,
Therefore he is held in esteem by all men.

LVII.

To govern a kingdom, use righteousness.
To conduct a war, use strategy.
To be a true world-ruler, be occupied with Inner
Life.

How do I know that this is so?
By this :—
   The more restrictive the laws,
      the poorer the people.
   The more machinery used,
      the more trouble in a kingdom.
   The more clever and skilful the people,
      the more do they make artificial things.
   The more the laws are in evidence,
      the more do thieves and robbers abound.

That is why the self-controlled man says :—
   If I act from Inner Life
      the people will become transformed in them-
      selves.
   If I love stillness
      the people will become righteous in them-
      selves.
   If I am occupied with Inner Life
      the people will become enriched in them-
      selves.
   If I love the Inner Life
      the people will become pure in themselves.

LVIII.

IF the government is from the heart
   the people will be richer and richer.
If the government is full of restrictions
   the people will be poorer and poorer.

Miserable ! you rely upon coming happiness.
Happy ! you crouch under dread of coming
   misery.
You may know the end from the beginning.

If a ruler is in line with Inner Life
   his strategy will come right,
   his bad luck will become good,
   and the people will be astonished.
   Things have been so for a long time.

That is why the self-controlled man
   is just and hurts no one,
   is disinterested and does no wrong,
   is true and takes no licence ;
   he shines, and offends not by his brightness.

LIX.

To govern men and to serve heaven
  nothing is better than to have a reserve.
The Master indeed has a reserve ;
  it is called brilliant foresight.
Brilliant foresight is called
  the increasing abundance of Teh.
If you have an ever-increasing abundance of Teh,
  then your Inner Life is unconquerable.
If your Inner Life is unconquerable,
  then its limits cannot be known.
If you cannot gauge the limits of your Inner Life,
  then you surely shall possess the kingdom.
If you possess the Mother of the kingdom,
  You shall endure for ever.
This is to be deep rooted
  and to have a firm foundation.
The possessor of Tao
  shall have enduring Life
  and infinite vision.

LX.

GOVERN a great State
As you would cook a small fish (do it gently).

When Tao is manifest in the world
Evil spirits have no power.

When evil spirits have no power
They cannot hurt men.

Evil spirits cannot hurt men.
The self-controlled man does not hurt men.
The Master also does not hurt men.
Therefore they unite in manifesting Teh.

LXI.

A GREAT kingdom, lowly like running water,
   is the Meeting-place of the world.
It is the feminine quality of the world.

The feminine quality always overcomes the
   masculine by stillness.
In order to be still, we must become lowly.

Therefore, if a great kingdom is lowly towards
      a little kingdom
   it will take possession of the little kingdom.
If a little kingdom is lowly towards a great
      kingdom
   it will take possession of the great kingdom.
So the one becomes lowly in order to conquer,
The other is lowly and yet it conquers.

If a great kingdom only desires to unify and
   nourish men,
If a small kingdom only desires to enter in and
   serve men,
Then the Master, in each case, shall obtain his
   desire.

He who is great ought to be lowly.

LXII.

HE who has the Tao is the refuge of all beings.
He is the treasure of the good man,
He is the support of the man who is not good.

Beautiful words through Tao gain power,
Man by following it gains steadfastness in action,
But, by the evil man, its possession is ignored.

The Son of Heaven sits enthroned,
His three Ministers are appointed.
One carries in his hand a tablet of jade ;
Another is followed by a mounted retinue.
But the one who is most valued
   sits quietly, and offers as his gift this Tao.

How was the Tao prized by men of Old ?
Daily they sought for it.
They found it, hid within the Self.
It gives a way of escape to the guilty.
Therefore it is prized by all men.

LXIII.

BE active, with the Activity of Inner Life.
Serve, with the Service of Inner Life.
Be fragrant, with the Fragrance of Inner Life.

The great shall be small,
The many shall be few, and
Evil shall be recompensed by goodness.

Meditate on difficult things till they become easy.
Do great deeds till they appear to be small.

To serve men in difficult things,
We must begin by easy things.
To serve men in great things,
We must begin by doing small things.

That is why the self-controlled man
　　to the end of life does not become great,
　　and thus he can perfect his greatness.

The Master has little faith in a quickly made
　　promise.
Many things are easy, many are also difficult.
The self-controlled man takes hold of difficulties.
To the end of life he solves difficulties in the
　　Inner Life.

LXIV.

HIS Restfulness is easily maintained.
Events foreseen by him are easily arranged for.
By him weak things are easily bent,
And small things are easily scattered.
He can stop an evil before it comes into existence.
He can keep a twig straight before it becomes
  crooked.

Behold the girth of this tree !
It grew from a small filament of a stalk.
This tower of nine storeys
  has its base upon a small space on the earth.
The journey of a thousand miles
  began with a single footstep on the ground.

He who makes, unmakes.
He who grasps, lets go.
That is why the self-controlled man
  by Inner Life can make and by Inner Life
    unmake,
  by Inner Life can grasp and by Inner Life
    let go.

Men in business affairs come near perfection,
  then fail.
If they were as attentive at the end as at the
  beginning their business would succeed.

That is why the self-controlled man
   desires to have no wishes ;
   he sets no value upon rare objects ;
   he learns without study ;
   he helps all beings by the outflow of his
      personality,
   and he does this without planning to do it.

NOTE on " the outflow of personality."—In the Notes
of Lecture VII. (Gifford Lectures, Edinburgh, 1914)
on " The Problem of Personality," Professor Henri
Bergson says :—" The human person is a being that is
capable of drawing out of himself more than is actually
there—a thing which is scarcely intelligible in the material
world, but which is real in the moral world. With a
slight effort of will we can draw indefinitely. It is within
the power of the person to expand, to increase, even
partially to create itself." A complementary statement
is made in " Christ in You," but in the latter quotation
we learn whence and in what measure comes the Force
that flows through the human person. " Just as much
as you yield to the Divine Innermost, in just the measure
that you live and bring forth the fruit of the Spirit, even
so shall you have access to all that Earth and Heaven
can yield." No one can prove this to another man ;
but each one of us can prove it by experience in our own
life.

LXV.

Of Old, he who was active in Tao
did not use it to make people enlightened,
but to make them more kind.

If people are difficult to govern
it is because they have too much knowledge.

Therefore if you govern a kingdom by knowledge,
you will be an oppressor of the kingdom.
But if you govern a kingdom by wisdom,
you will give happiness to the kingdom.

If you know and do these things
you will be a pattern for men.
Knowledge of how to be always a pattern for men
is called profound Teh.

Profound Teh is in the very source of life,
it pervades the utmost limits of life,
it returns and dwells in every being.

When fully manifested,
it unites all beings in a great harmony.

LXVI.

THE Rivers and the Seas (because they seek a
    lowly place)
  are Lords of a hundred valleys.
Let your love flow, seek a lowly place,
  you will be Lord of a hundred valleys.

That is why
  if the self-controlled man desires to exalt
    the people,
  in his speech he must take a lowly place;
  if he desires to put the people first,
  he must put himself after them.

Thus, though he dwells above them,
  the people are not burdened by him.
Though he is placed before them,
  the people are not obstructed by him,

Therefore men serve him gladly,
  they do not tire in serving him.
Because he does not strive,
  no one in the world can strive against him.

LXVII.

In the world many call me great,
  yet I seem to have no intelligence.
The Master indeed is great,
  yet he also seems to have no intelligence.
As regards our intelligence,
  its smallness is of long continuance.

The Master and I have three treasures,
We hold them and prize them.
The first is called "Deep Love,"
The second is called "Protectiveness,"
The third is called "Not planning to be first."

Having Deep Love, you then can have courage.
Having Protectiveness, you then can give freely.
Not planning to be first, you will be a perfect
  instrument that will endure.

Now, men neglect Deep Love and seek courage,
They put aside Protectiveness and seek extrava-
  gance,
They leave the second place and seek the first,
        Then death comes.

The Master fights by means of Love, then he
  conquers.
He keeps guard by means of it, then he is
  impregnable.
Heaven will save him, and by Love will defend him.

NOTE.—Compare :—

For never in the world does hatred cease by hatred ;
Hatred ceases by love ; this is always its nature.
                        —*Buddhist precept.*

LXVIII.

HE who loves, in being a soldier is not warlike.
He who loves, in fighting is not angry.
He who loves, in conquering does not grasp for self.
He who loves, in employing men is lowly before
them.

This is called Manifestation of non-greed.
It is called the power of using men.
It is called Unity with Heaven.
Of Old, it was man's highest aim.

LXIX.

A GREAT soldier used to say :—
"I plan not to be a Lord, but to be a follower ;
I plan not to advance an inch, but to recede a
foot."
This is called :—
Advancing with the advance of Inner Life,
baring the arm with the energy of Inner Life,
grasping a weapon with the force of Inner Life,
meeting the foe as a soldier of Inner Life.

There is no calamity greater than lightly to engage
in war.
To engage lightly in war is to lose our treasure
of gentleness.

Therefore, when soldiers meet who are equally
strong,
He who is compassionate shall conquer.

LXX.

My words are very easily known,
They are very easily practised.

No one in the world can fully know them,
No one in the world can fully practise them.

My words come from one Source,
My service is to one Ruler.

The Master indeed knows the Inner Kingdom,
That is why he knows the negation of self.

Few there are who know the self.
Because they know it not, they prize the self.

That is why the self-controlled man wears wool.
But in his bosom are jewels.

NOTE on "Negation."—The idea underlying the character for Negation 𣏾 is that of "a bird flying upwards and not coming down again" (Chalmers). This gives an inspiring picture of the soul forgetting the self with all its hampering habits and disabilities, and flying on the wings of faith to its home in the heavenly Inner Kingdom. What a futile word is "negation" to express this problem of self-adjustment.

LXXI.

To know that we are ignorant is a high attainment.
To be ignorant and to think we know is a defect.

The Master indeed can cure this defect.
That is why he has not this defect.

The self-controlled man has not this defect,
He takes hold of his defect and cures it.
That is why he has not this defect.

LXXII.

IF the people do not dread majesty,
Then great majesty will come to them.

Let them guard the innermost of their dwellings,
Let them press towards the innermost of their
　　life.

The Master indeed is not bound,
That is why he is not bound.

That is how the self-controlled man
  knows the Self
  and perceives the not-Self.
  He loves the Self,
  and honours the not-Self.

Therefore he passes away from the latter and
  takes hold of the former.

NOTE on " self " and " Self."—In Chapter 70 the
character that has been translated " self " 我 is
usually rendered " I," it is used as the first personal
pronoun, singular. It is composed of two characters,
手 meaning " hand " and 戈 " sword ". It repre-
sents a human personality, comprising body, emotions
and mind, the self of which Jesus spoke when He said
" Deny thyself, and follow Me." The idea of " hand "
and " sword " seems to be the conservation of personal
identity and rights. In Chapter 72 the character that
has been translated " Self " 自 , meaning the Higher
Self, the Divine-human being, is composed of two characters, at the left-hand side is the contraction for " man,"
and blent with it, the long stroke of " man " being an
integral part of its formation, is the character for " eye."
The eye is the human organ that links man with the
Universe, and is symbol of the Inner Vision that links
him consciously with God. In Chapter 70 we are told to
negate " self." In Chapter 72 we are told " to know the
Self and to perceive the not-Self ; to love the Self and to
honour the not-Self." The two selves must therefore be
harmonised and blent to make man an instrument fit
for Divine use.

LXXIII.

A MAN with courage and daring is slain,
A man with courage and self-restraint lives.

Of these two, the one has benefit, the other has
  injury.
Who can tell why one of them should incur
  Heaven's Wrath?
Because of this the self-controlled man has doubt
  and difficulty.

Heavenly Tao strives not, but conquers by Love ;
It speaks not, but responds in Love ;
It calls not to men, but of themselves they come ;
It slowly is made manifest, yet its plans are laid
  in Love.

The Net of Heaven
  is widely meshed, is widely meshed ;
  the meshes are far apart,
  yet nothing escapes from it.

LXXIV.

If the people do not fear death,
How then can you frighten them by death?

But if you cause the people continually to fear
    death,
And if one of them becomes a great criminal,
Can you take hold of him and slay him?

Would you dare to do this?
There is always one, the Executioner, who kills
    men.

But, on the contrary, if you kill as if you were
    Executioner,
It would be as if you tried to do the work of a
    Master Carpenter.

In attempting to do the work of a Master Carpenter,
Few there be who do not wound their own hands.

NOTE on "Capital Punishment."—T'ai Tsu, Founder
of the Ming Dynasty (1368 A.D.), in a preface to the
Tao Teh King, wrote thus :—" At the beginning of my
reign I had not yet learned the principles of the ancient
wise Kings. I questioned men about them, and they all
pretended to tell me. One day, while I was reading
through many books, I came across the *Tao Teh King*.
I found the style simple and the thoughts deep. After
some time I came upon this text :—' If the people do not
fear death, how, then, can you frighten them by death?'

At that time the Empire had only begun to be united; the people were obstinate, and the magistrates corrupt. Almost every morning ten men were executed in public; by the same evening a hundred others had committed the same crimes. Did not this justify the thought of Lao Tzŭ? From that time I ceased to inflict capital punishment. I imprisoned the guilty and imposed fines; and in less than a year my heart was comforted.

"I recognised then that in this book is the perfect source of all things. It is the sublime Master of Kings, and the inestimable treasure of the people."

—From *Julien's Notes*.

LXXV.

THE people are hungry.
Because they who are over the food tax it heavily
That is why the people are hungry.

The people are difficult to govern.
Because the rulers trust in possessions and activities,
That is why the people are difficult to govern.

The people make light of death.
Because they work hard in order to save their life,
That is why they make light of death.

A Master indeed is he whose life-activities are from within.
He excels all men in his appreciation of Life.

LXXVI.

In life, man is soft and tender,
In death he is rigid and hard.

In life, plants and trees are soft and pliant,
In death they are withered and tough.

Thus rigidity and hardness are companions of
    death.
Softness and tenderness are companions of life.

That is why the soldier who trusts only in strength
    does not conquer,
The tree that relies on its strength invites the
    axe.

Great strength dwells below,
Softness and tenderness dwell above.

LXXVII.

HEAVENLY Tao is like the bending of a bow.
That which is high is bent downwards,
That which is low is raised up,
That which is too much is lessened,
That which is not enough is increased.

Heavenly Tao takes from those who have too
  much,
And gives to those who have not enough.

The way of man is not thus.
He takes from those who have not enough,
And gives to those who already have too much.

Who is able to hold his wealth in order to give
  it to men?
Only he who has the Tao.

That is why the self-controlled man
  acts without looking for reward,
    he brings to perfectness without claiming
      credit,
    he desires not to let his wisdom appear.

LXXVIII.

Of the soft and weak things in the world
None is weaker than water.
But in overcoming that which is firm and strong
Nothing can equal it.

It is easy to know the inner meaning of this :
    " That which is weak conquers the strong,
    That which is soft conquers the hard."

All men know this,
No one is able to practise it.

That is why the self-controlled man says :—
    " He who bears the reproach of the Kingdom
    is called Ruler of the Land.
    He who bears the woes of the Kingdom
    is called King of the land."

True words in paradox.

LXXIX.

To harmonise great enemies
We must possess that which far surpasses enmity.

We must be able to be at peace
In order to be active in Love.

That is why the self-controlled man
  holds the left-hand portion of the contract,
  but does not insist upon the other man producing
    his portion.

He who is virtuous may rule by a contract,
He whose virtue is within may rule by destroying
  it.

Akin to Heavenly Tao is Inner Life.
A constant giver is the man who loves.

NOTE.—The tablet upon which a contract was written
was broken into two pieces, each party retaining a piece.
At the settlement the contract was carried through only
if the portions fitted accurately. The man who is
" active in Love " keeps to his bargain without insisting
upon this formality.

—See *Julien's Notes.*

LXXX.

TAKE a small kingdom and few people,
Cause ten or a hundred of them to carry weapons,
But not to use them.

Cause the people to fear death,
Do not let them travel far,
Though they may have boats and carriages,
Let them use them only within the kingdom.
Though they may have soldiers in uniform,
Let them parade only within the kingdom.
Cause the people again to have knotted cords,
And to use them (instead of the written character).

Their food would be sweet,
Their clothing would be beautiful in their own
    eyes,
Their dwellings would be resting-places,
They would love simple ways.

If another kingdom were so near
That they could hear the sounds of dogs and fowls,
They would not come into mutual contact
Until they all grew old and died.

For NOTE on this Chapter see Introduction, pp. 12, 13.

LXXXI.

FAITHFUL words may not be beautiful,
Beautiful words may not be faithful.

Those who love do not quarrel,
Those who quarrel do not love.

Those who know are not learned,
Those who are learned do not know.

The riches of the self-controlled man are in the
    Inner Life.
When he spends for others, he has more for
    himself.
When he gives to others, he has much more for
    himself.

Heavenly Tao blesses all and hurts no one.

The way of the self-controlled man is to act and
    not to fight.

NOTE on " knowing " and " learning."—Learning is
a faculty of the intellect ; knowing is a faculty of the
intuition. Learning, thought, activity of the mind are
like our daylight, by which we are able to accommodate
ourselves to our temporal environment. Knowledge,
perception, apprehension by the intuition are like our
starlight, by means of which we may come to realise our

place in the immensity of the Universe. Bergson says :— "We have the power of apprehending reality without the limitations that the intellect imposes ; in the intuition of life we see reality as it is " (" Philosophy of Change," by H. Wildon Carr). Learning is like the accumulation of facts about a friend. You may collect them, tabulate them, and store them in the memory ; then you may say :—" I know my friend, I have learned all about him." But how different is the knowledge that is gained by one look into his eyes, by the perception that comes through contact, by the mysterious flow of his personality of which you are aware when he is near you. Knowing him thus, you may say :—" I know my friend really as he is." The latter is a life-process. It is by such a life-process that we may return into Tao, that we may know God, to know Whom is Life Eternal. " By love may He be gotten and holden ; but by thought never."

THE END.